MW01206321

This note book belongs to :

Date:

Made in the USA
Las Vegas, NV
18 March 2022

45932567R00059